The Revenue
Marketing Book

INDIA • SINGAPORE • MALAYSIA

Notion Press

Old No. 38, New No. 6
McNichols Road, Chetpet
Chennai - 600 031

First Published by Notion Press 2020
Copyright © Yaagneshwaran Ganesh 2020
All Rights Reserved.

ISBN 978-1-64892-619-8

This book has been published with all efforts taken to make the material error-free after the consent of the author. However, the author and the publisher do not assume and hereby disclaim any liability to any party for any loss, damage, or disruption caused by errors or omissions, whether such errors or omissions result from negligence, accident, or any other cause.

While every effort has been made to avoid any mistake or omission, this publication is being sold on the condition and understanding that neither the author nor the publishers or printers would be liable in any manner to any person by reason of any mistake or omission in this publication or for any action taken or omitted to be taken or advice rendered or accepted on the basis of this work. For any defect in printing or binding the publishers will be liable only to replace the defective copy by another copy of this work then available.

The Revenue Marketing Book

How to build a predictable
and repeatable revenue
marketing engine that works

Yaagneshwaran Ganesh

Foreword by Pravin Shekar & Last word by Christian Fictoor

INDIA · SINGAPORE · MALAYSIA

IN)ICACADEMY

INDIC PLEDGE

———❦❦———

- *I celebrate our civilisational identity, continuity & legacy in thought, word and deed.*

- *I believe our indigenous thought has solutions for the global challenges of health, happiness, peace, and sustainability.*

- *I shall seek to preserve, protect and promote this heritage in doing so,*
  - *discover, nurture and harness my potential,*
  - *connect, cooperate and collaborate with fellow seekers,*
  - *be inclusive and respectful of diverse opinions.*

ABOUT INDIC ACADEMY

———❦❦———

Indic Academy is a non-traditional 'university' for traditional knowledge. We seek to bring about a global renaissance based on Indic civilizational and indigenous thought. We are pursuing a multidimensional strategy across time, space and cause by establishing centers of excellence, transforming intellectuals and building an ecosystem.

Indic Academy is pleased to support this book.

*This book and almost everything else that
I do would be impossible without the unconditional
support of my wife, Aarthi.*

To her, and my two beautiful children

– Vidyut and Anjana.

CONTENTS

Part III: Optimizing Your Revenue Marketing Journey

Part IV: Bonus Chapter

PRAISE FOR THE BOOK

"The success of the modern B2B marketing team will be evaluated by the revenue impact it delivers to the company and Yaag has laid out a crisp and compelling model on how to transform marketing into a revenue-generating team."

– Jeff Davis, Founder and Principal, JD2 Consulting and award-winning author of 'Create Togetherness'

"The Revenue Marketing Book is a worthwhile read for entrepreneurs and marketers who are intent on making their marketing efforts translate into revenue."

– Scott Brinker, Editor at chiefmartec.com & the Chair of Martech Conference

"A must-read operating manual for marketers who want to deliver exponential revenue."

– Sangram Vajre, Author, Co-founder at Terminus, and the host of #FlipMyFunnel, a top 50 business podcast in the world.

"All your marketing channels, properties and activities are a waste of time unless they contribute to revenue. Yaag's book gives you an approach to make your marketing count."

– Vinod Muthukrishnan, Chief Growth Officer at Cisco

"A new way to look at marketing to finally be able to give some ROI to this intangible business function. Yaag's insights make 'The Revenue Marketing Book' a practical and meaningful point of reference."

– Claire Boscq-Scott, Global CX Guru and CEO at the BusyQueenBee

FOREWORD

Money talks, bullshit walks

Entrepreneurs, we have seen them all. We know of CEOs who go about their work without much fuss while some others who insist on shouting from rooftops about every move they make. There are those who go up and down and up again, and then there are those who go up and up, and down and out!

In the course of my long career as an entrepreneur and outlier marketer, I have interacted with over a 1000 CEOs. It is a roller coaster ride that we have happily signed up for, with clear intention.

Yes, there is quite some glamour associated with calling ourselves an "entrepreneur". As with all initiatives and relationships, the honeymoon period does come to a halt. And that is when reality strikes.

Am I making money?

That is the question Yaagneshwaran Ganesh has addressed in this book. I have followed Yaag's work over the past few years and he is a marketer who focuses on the basics and speaks his mind. He has done the same in the "The Revenue Marketing Book".

'Are you bringing in revenue?'

It is a simple yes or no question.

Well, it is easy to duck behind the ocean of grey that most mediocre marketers and entrepreneurs tend to hide behind. You may often hear them say, "You know I've worked so hard in my business". "If only my customers understood my product". "Why don't they get it". "Do you know the number of Facebook likes I have?". "I am the buzz of the town. Everyone is talking about me!".

Vanity metrics are good for the ego in short doses. But that does not make them a medicine that cures all ills. It is not an invincibility cloak.

A business starts with only one objective – to provide significant returns to the stakeholders. Your product or service should provide a solution that your client needs or wants. It should be a solution that the client is ready and willing to pay for.

In today's business world, revenue marketing is the much-required common sense for entrepreneurs.

So, whose responsibility is it to generate revenue?

Everyone!

Everyone should focus on generating revenue and fine-tuning the processes to optimize the profits.

Why does revenue marketing matter? How can you and your team build a revenue marketing engine that works?

Invest the 45 minutes it takes to read this book in one go. Then, use the book to discuss with your team and build a predictable recurring revenue engine.

Thank you,

Pravin Shekar

Outlier Marketer

INTRODUCTION

Alright, let's get straight to the point.

It doesn't matter how sophisticated your martech stack is, what your marketing budget is, or how many people you have in your marketing organization. You must know what is contributing to revenue (directly or indirectly), what is working, and what needs to be done away with.

Many managers think that a great marketing campaign that supports a great product will always work. It is not necessarily so.

It isn't uncommon to see the biggest of brands betting on big-budget marketing campaigns without being able to attribute it to any tangible outcome. You see them spending millions of dollars on party-crashing a competitor's mega-event, flying a blimp, and more.

Yes, it does capture eyeballs. Yes, it gets you PR. But what does it translate into? Does it help in customer acquisition?

Well, it may.

But the question is — is the outcome measurable? Are we able to predict the revenue outcome?

In fact, according to the Pragmatic Institute, roughly 85% of B2B marketers are feeling intense pressure to add direct revenue accountability to their job description.

We don't even have to debate on this. Your real-time proof is just one LinkedIn search away. Until a few years ago, there were very few companies that had revenue-based titles in the marketing department. But now, a quick search on LinkedIn will spit out a lot of people with revenue marketing titles.

So, what is revenue marketing? How does it change the life of a marketer?

Fundamentally, revenue marketing is an attempt to move marketing from being a cost center to a revenue center. The core of revenue marketing is — to be able to build a repeatable set of processes and programs to drive customer acquisition and recurring revenue.

Therefore, it isn't just about top of the funnel activities or driving product signups, but also about improving revenue per customer with customer marketing, upselling and cross-selling programs.

What makes it interesting is the need to build a predictable revenue flow into the organization.

And that is possible only if you can map the marketing activities to specific revenue objectives, and thereby a specific revenue outcome.

If it is so obvious, why isn't it the norm?

Because — it isn't as easy as it sounds. It is because a prospect's journey isn't a linear one. For instance, a prospect doesn't move from demand generation to product marketing to sales enablement to sales anymore. The movement is random.

So, how do you map every marketing activity and investment to a revenue outcome? How do you set up your marketing organization for a seamless revenue marketing journey?

That is what this book delves into. While making no claims on this book being the only gold standard to set up your revenue marketing journey, I promise to make this book worthy of your time by keeping it simple, practical and actionable.

Welcome to The Revenue Marketing Book.

With great revenue responsibility, comes great marketing.

#revenuemarketingbook

THE TLDR VERSION OF THE BOOK

Marketers have the shortest tenure in the C-Suite. The value we create needs to become more tangible, measurable and presentable in terms of revenue. Regardless of whether you are in the beginning of your marketer careers or well experienced, the expectations from you are going to be continuously on the rise.

So...

Align to the revenue goals.

Ask the right questions, set up the right process.

Invest on the right avenues.

Do not waste marketing money.

Measure what matters, with context and purpose.

No more vanity metrics.

Iterate, reiterate

Keep delivering value.

Be the no-fluff, all-stuff revenue marketer!

PART I

WHY DOES REVENUE MARKETING MATTER?

1. DON'T WAIT UNTIL YOU ARE READY

....

*There never has to be a difference between
who you are and what you do*

– Gary Vaynerchuck

Yes! You read that right. You don't have to wait until you are ready to get started with the revenue marketing journey.

You don't need a 25-member marketing team or separate marketing teams for SEO, growth, product marketing, PR, etc. to make your marketing measurable or aligned to revenue.

There have been organizations where I was the only marketing person in the entire company, where I played the role of the CMO, content writer, SEO professional, PR person, and sometimes even sales. The point I'm trying to make here is - you don't need a big team or too many activities or even a well-oiled marketing engine to get started with revenue marketing.

You are ready. You always were.

You just need to start making it count.

You might think your marketing isn't mature enough compared to some of the other companies you compete with. That is natural, and good awareness to have.

At the same time, let it not get you into the 'impostor syndrome.'[1] For instance, if you are just starting up don't set unreasonable goals or don't compare yourself with companies that have been in the industry for more than ten years. If you do so, you will only end up getting disappointed.

Embrace your situation, know where you stand. Just get started and set up realistic and measurable goals. Set goals that contribute to revenue.

The idea of revenue marketing is simply being able to map marketing activities, engagements, and touchpoints to revenue outcomes. So, if you are a small team or even a one-member team, it makes even more sense to focus only on the marketing activities that impact the bottom line.

Revenue marketing isn't about big teams or small teams. It's about driving revenue with your marketing initiatives. At the core of it, you need to be able to build a repeatable set of processes and programs to drive customer acquisition and recurring revenue. There are two key words here - 'repeatable' and 'recurring revenue.'

Therefore, it is more than top of the funnel marketing activities or driving product signups. It is about improving revenue per customer, finding opportunities to upsell and cross-sell, and most importantly reduce customer churn.

If you have a small team - brilliant! Make it count.

If you have a big team - excellent! Align towards revenue outcome, drive accountability.

It doesn't matter what your current marketing or martech maturity is. Don't let where you are, stop where you want to be.

---

1 Impostor syndrome is a psychological phenomenon in which people are unable to internalize their accomplishments or capabilities.

Acknowledge where you are, but also set your eyes on where you need to be.

Everyone must start somewhere, let's start here and now.

Accountability is everything. What you account for, you deliver.

#revenuemarketingbook

2. REPUTATION, RELATIONSHIP AND REVENUE

....

There is nothing more valuable than a spotless reputation.

William Shakespeare

Imagine yourself walking across the aisles of a supermarket. Take a look at the items you have added to your cart. How many of those items come from a brand you didn't know before?

Very few, right?

Similarly, when you buy a CRM software — whom would you invest on? A known and trusted brand or would it be one of the million CRMs you have never heard of?

Known brand, right? Then as marketers, why do we expect people to consume our content and instantly go on to sign-up for our product, and become our customers for life, even before building our brands?

Brands put in a lot of effort over years to become the brands we choose. Let's take content as one of the contributors to brand building. It is a chicken and egg problem. You would trust content coming only from the likes of a Gartner or Forrester or reputed brands like Hubspot or Salesforce. But to establish that trust, they had to deliver great content consistently over a long period.

But who has the time? Across the globe, the average job tenure for a CMO, especially in the tech world, is about 26 months.

One of the key reasons for that is the ineffectiveness to prove value quantitatively. It's the era of instant gratification.

© YAAGNESHWARAN GANESH

There are three Rs that contribute to marketing success:

+ Reputation
+ Relationship
+ Revenue Enablement

It'll boil down to how you contribute in the three Rs.

Reputation: It is all about setting up the brand as a trusted product or service provider in the industry. It comprises factors such as aligning the positioning of the product with the overarching positioning of the company, capturing mindshare and market share for the product category.

So, ask yourself — how are you leveraging thought leadership to build awareness and drive engagement? Can you add value to your target audience with deal-specific content that includes playbooks, battle cards, videos, and other engaging assets to improve trust?

Relationship: How you drive reach and engagement with your target audience, how you build 1:1 relationship with stakeholders within your organization, customers, industry thought leaders, and analysts.

Can you work closely with your product teams, sales teams, customer support, and customer success teams to incorporate the right message that resonates with your customers? Can you play a role in establishing a Customer Advisory Board (CAB)? A CAB can be of great help in helping you differentiate your product from the competition and sometimes even help you directly or indirectly in winning large deals

Revenue Enablement: This is the most important one. In fact, the previous two Rs are also tied to this. What's the point of reputation if it doesn't translate into revenue? Why would a customer maintain a relationship with your brand if he/she are not invested in your product or services?

So, it comes to this — how are you contributing to the existing pipeline? How are you contributing to the net new revenue? Are you contributing towards increasing the pipeline velocity? Are you contributing towards decreasing customer churn?

The lifetime of a marketer in a company is now directly related to the impact he/she had on the revenue. As their seniority and experience grow, the expectation to contribute to the revenue increases exponentially.

And, if you are beginning your career in marketing — make sure you align your operations to revenue right away.

There is no better time to become a revenue marketer than now.

The good thing about this is — the path to revenue marketing won't be boring. It is going to be a journey of failure, discovery, need for grit and perseverance to track things that matter until you see the revenue numbers achieved against your name and get recognized for it.

It will seem like a painted canvas that leaves art-lovers in awe — and yet you will pick up the targets for the next quarter, or next year and get to your act straight.

It will happen again; it will continuously evolve. Yet, as it happens, we will be excited and wonder why our eyes are wide and our jaws are on the floor.

One thing for sure — the journey is worth it.

*You'll find everything about marketing
to be worthwhile, if it contributes to
a meaningful outcome.*

#revenuemarketingbook

3. BUT, WHY REVENUE MARKETING?

To build a long-term, successful enterprise,
when you don't close a sale, open a relationship.

– Patricia Fripp

The marketing world is full of jargons and buzzwords. It is not uncommon to see age old concepts with subtle tweaks being brought back with new names and a bunch of reports and PR around it.

Is revenue marketing another such buzzword? Not really.

It is fundamental. It is as simple as answering the question — are you as a marketer contributing to revenue or not?

Let's understand the significance of this question, and why is it at the heart of marketing?

Try answering this as honestly as possible:

If you were to bootstrap a startup and didn't have access to a lot of funds, who would you hire? A Sales Development Representative (SDR) who builds his or her own prospect list and revenue pipeline with minimum investments such as a phone, a laptop and a LinkedIn Sales Navigator account?

(or)

Would it be a content writer who produces quality content, which would then take its own time to get website traffic and then lead a fraction of those readers to request a demo of your product or sign up for trial?

You would want to bet on the first option, right?

While the idea isn't to take anything away from content marketing or pay per click (PPC) ads, it is to show that you as a founder always will go by what gives quicker returns with minimal risk. Similarly, if you are an investor — you want to bet on the company that is on the growth path. The one that gives you 5x-10x returns.

Today's CEO's aren't happy with the leads and the metrics related to them. Their eyes are on the prize — revenue. What matters is the potential pipeline value created by you.

© YAAGNESHWARAN GANESH

Several surveys already indicate that since the beginning of 2020, there has been a 7.5% increase in the number of B2B marketing organizations that started holding their marketers accountable for pipeline/ revenue contribution compared to 2019.

It augurs well for those organizations because both the marketers and sales folks are incentivised to work towards the same goal. It is important for more organizations to go down this path.

One of the primary reasons why sales and marketing teams are at loggerheads is because sales teams don't see value in the leads shared by the marketing teams. Marketing teams feel that sales teams don't give a damn about the leads shared with them.

In fact, Manish Nepal (my good friend, co-host at The ABM Conversations Podcast and a content marketing expert) and I did a #coffeeconversations episode on the topic – Why do sales and marketing teams collide?

In that episode, we discussed – when sales teams receive a bunch of leads, they want the leads to be sales ready. They want the leads to move to the next stage of the funnel and ultimately convert into deals. And that almost never happens.

(Note: If you are interested in watching to that episode, here's the link to it - https://www.linkedin.com/posts/yaagneshwarang_

coffeeconversations-productmarketing-b2bmarketing-activity-6604606666082172928-fh8a)

The reason it never happens is because the goals of marketing and sales teams aren't aligned. Marketers are measured on KPIs such as number of leads generated, cost per click, etc. whereas the sales teams are measured by revenue generated.

Unfortunately, for a long time, marketing has never been responsible for revenue. If we marketers want to add value and contribute to the organization's growth, we have to take up revenue ownership.

Sooner or later, revenue contribution will become the factor that determines the lifetime of a marketer in an organization.

Interestingly, several organizations are already taking steps in this direction. They are tying marketers' compensation to revenue generation in the form of variable pay.

For a long time — variable pay components were common only for sales teams. But now, marketing is about building predictable revenue.

If you are a marketer who can measure ROI from your marketing budget and contribute to revenue, you put yourself and your organization on the growth path.

*You don't matter, if you aren't contributing
to the things that matter.*

#revenuemarketingbook

4. HIPS DON'T LIE, AND BLIMPS DON'T FLY!

You can run but you can't hide.

– Emily Giffin

We all have heard Shakira's 'Hips don't lie' at some point, but why is it relevant here? What does it mean in the marketing context?

We're talking about revenue and expenses. One thing that never lies is your balance sheet. It is a single pane of glass that tells you how your company is performing. For instance, a quick look at your burn rate and cash reserve would tell you whether your company can be self-sustaining or if you need to be raising capital soon.

For starters, burn rate refers to the rate at which your company spends cash. It is usually calculated on a monthly basis. But in some critical situations, it may be measured in days or weeks.

So, now your balance sheet doesn't lie, and you know your burn rate. What next?

Apply the good old OODA loop. OODA stands for Observe, Orient, Decide, Act.

In the simplest terms, it means - know what has happened, ask "so what" and decide "now what".

Contextually, this means - know what your marketing expenses are, what is the return on expense, and then decide where you need to continue spending and where to stop..

For example, if your monthly marketing expense is $10000, make a list of channels on which the marketing dollars are spent.

Let's say, $3000 goes into Facebook ads, then analyse the outcome from it. Don't stop with the number of impressions or click throughs - analyze the number of signups or demo requests you received, analyze the potential revenue pipeline built. Then decide whether it makes sense to invest elsewhere, or double down your investment on Facebook ads by taking away the budget from a channel that is not delivering the desired results.

This isn't rocket science, and yet you often see that burn rates are a huge issue with some companies. You can't complain either, because these are companies that typically go after customer mindshare, and more importantly compete with industry leaders. And if you are a startup competing in that zone, you are going to burn cash for a long time before you finally start making revenue in a profitable way.

But most companies cannot afford that. Founders want revenue, profit, and sustainability. They want to put food on the table. So, as a marketer — your primary job is to create avenues for revenue.

At this point, some of you might think — the primary role of a marketer is to build awareness, engagement, create value, and trust.

All that is true and the only way to measure the trust, value, and awareness created is its translation in opportunities and revenue. That said, the impact needn't always be direct revenue. It can also be outcomes that indirectly impact revenue, such as number of signups for your product, requests for demos, reducing customer churn, and more.

© YAAGNESHWARAN GANESH

So, what's the first step towards revenue marketing?

Flying blimps at iconic conferences and crashing parties of industry leaders? Definitely no. These things may get you attention and are PR worthy too, but how do you map the outcome to revenue?

To an extent, you can attribute the increase in traffic, but it's tough to attribute the number of sign-ups from this source and thereby the revenue.

You need to ensure that revenue is the ultimate goal of every marketing activity across the company. So, the next thing to look at is, what is the motivation for each marketer in your company?

Look at the Key Result Areas (KRA) sheet of a marketer and it will give you an understanding of the marketing segment they belong to in the company. For instance, if someone's KRAs are in the area of PR, corporate communications, you know they are aligned to corporate marketing. Similarly, the ones aligned with product marketing have KRAs related to on-boarding, product adoption, etc.

But the key question is how does each team contribute to revenue? Do the KPIs and KRAs of one team help the other? For instance, a marketing team might be happy if an email campaign had a high click-through rate, but it may mean nothing to the sales team.

Sales teams want prospects that are highly engaged and sales ready. You need everyone to be aligned to achieve a collective outcome.

To sum up, the balance sheet doesn't lie. If your marketing doesn't have a direct or indirect impact on revenue, your time and efforts are better off on something that moves the needle.

Three things cannot be hidden — the sun,
the moon and the worthiness of a marketing team.

#revenuemarketingbook

PART II

BUILDING YOUR REVENUE
MARKETING ENGINE

5. REVENUE BINDS YOUR ORGANIZATION

Marketing is not anyone's job... It's everyone's job!

– Jack Welch

Every company tries to tell their customers that they are customer-first. Some of them go a little bolder and even say "customers for life". Brilliant! So what?

Yes, these companies truly seem to believe in the ideology, and the walls look great with the framed posters carrying the message. But how much of it is true?

Let's uncomplicate that question.

How many of us who call ourselves 'customer first' have really structured our organizations towards that? Does your marketing, sales, customer success, and customer support teams work as one team?

Or let's just try to answer this honestly — has the revenue per customer increased or decreased in the last one year? How many customers are churning away every month?

Because, being close to the customer isn't enough anymore. Having the best product or service isn't enough either. Neither is it about being the best brand nor having the best story.

It is a combination of all the above.

In short, it's not enough to own the supply.
You need to own the demand.

To be able to drive market demand, you need to have a common binding factor that drives your marketing, sales, customer support, and customer success teams.

And that is revenue.

If revenue can be made the common goal for these teams, you are potentially setting a flywheel in motion. In fact, more and more companies are already measuring their marketing teams based on their contribution to revenue.

Here's a dipstick to that: Until a few years ago, there were very few companies that had revenue-based titles in the marketing department. But if you do a quick search on LinkedIn now, you will come across a lot many people with revenue marketing titles on their profiles.

The best part about setting a common goal is that the outcome of one's marketing efforts feeds in as input for another team. In fact, the goal setting in mature marketing organizations tend to start with revenue goals and are then worked backwards to arrive at the marketing programs and KPIs to get there.

For instance, let's take content marketing as a case.

The purpose of content marketing is beyond producing and distributing great content. You need to tie your content marketing efforts to the outcome your sales team is looking for and what it eventually brings in.

The Forrester graphic below provides a great example.

FORRESTER RESEARCH | B2B MARKETING PROFESSIONALS

Measure Content Marketing Value In Four Dimensions: Content, Audience, Sales, And Business
Make Sales Efficiency A Key Addition To Your B2B Content Marketing Metrics

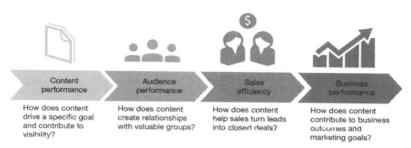

Content performance	Audience performance	Sales efficiency	Business performance
How does content drive a specific goal and contribute to visibility?	How does content create relationships with valuable groups?	How does content help sales turn leads into closed deals?	How does content contribute to business outcomes and marketing goals?

128821   Source: Forrester Research, Inc. Unauthorized reproduction, citation, or distribution prohibited.

The feedback on the contribution to revenue outcome is super critical, which is often easily missed.

If you look at it, content marketing is one of the teams that often tend to work in silos (in most companies). On one side, the sales teams aren't always aware of the latest sales enablement content available, whereas the content writers don't know what type of content converts at each stage of the funnel.

It would make a lot of sense to analyze content consumption and conversion patterns at the top of the funnel, mid-funnel and bottom funnel. You need to know the kind of content consumed by the decision makers, influencers and the users of your product.

More importantly, you need to know what piece of content moved the needle at each level — so that you can focus on creating content that converts and thereby contributes to revenue.

The idea of having revenue as the binding factor is not just for the content team, but for the entire organization. In short, you get rewarded if you can measure the impact throughout the stages of the funnel and prove value for your campaigns, technology investments, and hires.

In the next chapter, let's look at how to set up the revenue marketing journey.

Unless all the teams come together to collaborate towards a common purpose, there's no progress.

#revenuemarketingbook

6. SETTING UP THE REVENUE MARKETING JOURNEY

Even though you are on the right track,
you'll get run over if you just sit there.

– Will Rogers

With marketing becoming more and more tech-driven, it has now become far more feasible to measure and track how campaigns perform in terms of customer acquisition. And as organizations get more sophisticated, revenue marketing drives the sales pipeline.

In fact, alignment with sales is increasingly becoming a factor in the compensation of marketers. It is observed that marketing teams closely aligned with sales outcomes tend to have higher compensation compared to those whose sales alignment isn't clearly pronounced.

With that said, a study contributing to the CaliberMind State of Revenue Marketing report 2020[2] suggests that 60% of marketers can't measure or are unsure of their ROI.

---

2 State of Revenue Marketing Report: https://www.calibermind.com/state-of-revenue-marketing-report-2020

© YAAGNESHWARAN GANESH

So, when you go about building your revenue marketing engine, you need to:

1. Focus the entire journey and programs based on revenue impact

2. Make sure your sales, customer support, and customer success works as one team to drive revenue

3. Leverage martech efficiently and effectively, i.e. don't buy subscriptions for a ton of tools that are never used by your team.

4. Understand the current skills available, identify skills needed

5. Set up the right KPIs and accountabilities to your team members

It all starts with understanding where you are in terms of revenue marketing maturity, where do you want to be (by when?), what do you need to get there, and then getting into the execution cycle.

To understand where you are - the Revenue Marketing Maturity stages in the table below will give you a good overview of the different maturity levels

Traditional	Lead Generation	Demand Generation	Revenue Marketing
Marketing as party planner and cost center	Marketing became little more tactical - emails for lead gen	Marketing became automated with introduction of martech	Martech to map the entire customer journey and revenue attribution
Focused on brand building and awareness	Focused on optimizing cost per lead	Focused on MQL, SQL and optimizing the funnel	Focused on building revenue predictability and a repeatable process
Not even generating leads	Generated leads but not aligned with sales pursuits	Aligned with sales, yet lot of disagreements on lead quality	Aligned with sales, customer support and customer success as revenue team
Accounted for expense and campaigns	**Accounted for expense and lead gen activites**	**Started accounting for costs and revenue pipeline**	**Accountable for revenue generated, ROI and revenue forecast**

*Table concept improvised based on The Pedowitz Revenue Marketing Journey

And as you get into the mode of what you need to do to move to the next stage and get into the execution mode, it is extremely important to acknowledge the core decision makers and contributors and the roles they will play.

Let us look at some of the key people involved and their responsibilities in getting your revenue engine up and running.

Director or VP of Revenue Marketing: The primary responsibilities of the person in this role is to strategize demand generation and deploy a scalable revenue marketing architecture. It means the person in this role directs the team on the channels to engage with prospects and customers and oversee the lead funnel, makes sure campaigns are directly aligned to building the pipeline, and thereby create revenue impact.

Contribution to revenue marketing: They help the organization move away from the traditional way of measuring customer acquisition cost (CAC) to measuring CAC per channel. It means – traditionally organizations measure CAC with the generic formula:

CAC = Total expense on acquiring customers / number of customers acquired.

Measuring CAC per channel helps you figure out the most cost-effective channel contributing to revenue. The Director or VP of Revenue Marketing is often measured by revenue generated per dollar spent, length of sales cycle and profitability margin on revenue generated.

Marketing Analyst: The title "Marketing Analyst" is a loosely used term by a lot of organizations around the world. In this context, the focus of the role is to measure campaign analytics over time and constantly review the numbers. This role is super critical because of the shift from campaign efficiency metrics such as opens and CTRs to revenue metrics such as signups effected, and so on.

Contribution to revenue marketing: They measure campaign effectiveness in terms of revenue outcome. Their reports don't talk about the number of leads generated, but instead talk about the potential revenue pipeline created. Their key objective is to share insights on conversion opportunities and are often measured on

1) Improvement percentage in conversion across each stage of the funnel

2) Number of customers who are in free plans/packages who upgraded to premium/paid plans.

Marketing Technologist: Technology is at the heart of revenue marketing. On an average, the mid-size firms tend to have 20-25% of their budget assigned for martech investments. So, the person in this role needs to be sure of what the must-haves are. For instance, if you must run an effective ABM campaign, you need all the infrastructure set up from predictive intelligence, the right CRM, marketing automation, content distribution tools, analytical tools, and more. Yet, the marketing technologist must make sure that they do not have any tools that are not effectively adopted across the organization.

Contribution to revenue marketing: The role of the marketing technologist is to play the role of a power user when it comes to running campaigns and thereby continuously contribute to refine the revenue metrics according to the business needs.

They are often measured based on the measurability of marketing outcomes, and the quality and trustability of data across the organization, delivering a single version of truth.

Content marketers: Content will always remain the king even if the content formats keep changing and evolving. You need the right creatives and copies that lead to conversions, be it emails, websites, landing pages, ebooks, or more. You need quality content marketers who not only produce quality content but also distribute the content effectively to build awareness, interest, consideration and conversion. The key is to make sure that the content is customer-centric and not product-centric. Customers should be able to resonate with it.

Contribution to revenue marketing: The key here is to make sure that the type of content is clearly mapped to the specific parts of the funnel. For instance, you want content that caters to awareness creation at the top of the funnel, whereas you provide access to customer case studies to a prospect in the consideration stage and competition comparison battlecards with someone in the decision-making stage, and so on. Thus, the role of content marketers in revenue marketing is to enable trust building at each stage of the funnel and accelerate their funnel progress. The effectiveness of content marketing is measured by the conversion affected by the content at each stage. The conversion here can range from expressing interest for a product demo to request to talk to sales.

To sum up, the key is to set up your marketing operations in such a way that every team and every team member contributes to revenue, which is measurable and attributable. If you can manage that, and continuously improve every moving part, you end up setting the revenue marketing flywheel in motion – from strategy to execution to revenue.

If you need to explain to people in your company about how marketing adds value, you probably haven't added value yet.

#revenuemarketingbook

7. THE REVENUE MARKETING FRAMEWORK

It is the method behind the madness that makes it madness.

– Marty Rubin

One of the primary steps in aligning marketing operations to deliver revenue is to make sure that everyone has a clear understanding of their KRA. Unless one has clarity on his/her KRA, people will end up working in silos.

Here are a few examples of gaps you might come across in organizations where marketing and sales teams tend to work in silos:

1. Marketers stick to good old methods of what worked for them in the past and don't experiment enough to stay relevant in the ever-changing business scenarios.

2. Sales and marketing not being aligned. For instance, the sales teams don't communicate the essence of customer conversations with the marketing teams (which could be of great value in creating relevant messaging or even tweaking the product positioning).

To avoid silos and contribute to revenue in a synchronized manner, here's a revenue marketing framework I came up with. I call it "The GAME Model".

It stands for Gather ---> Agree ---> Map ---> Execute.

The idea of the GAME model originated while mentoring a software startup in the Netherlands in January 2019. We were in the process of identifying why the revenue per customer was so low despite the efforts from their marketing and sales teams.

In the process, we identified a few key factors that contributed to deal size and closure. Finally, we arrived at a four-step process where marketing and sales teams could work as one unit to help the customer achieve their goals and thereby directly contribute to the organization's revenue.

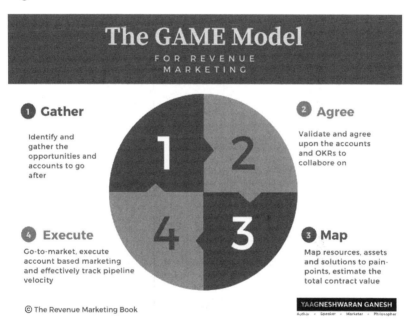

I. Gather

✦ Invest your time and energies to identify the accounts you want to spend your marketing dollars and efforts on. It is not necessary that the accounts you want to go after should be net new accounts.

✦ As marketers, we shouldn't miss out on marketing to existing customers, where we can 'land and expand' the opportunities within an account.

✦ Identify the marketing sources that contribute to revenue such as content, PPC, events, etc. and the areas of collaboration with the sales team such as delivering the right case studies, competitor comparison sheets, ROI calculators, solution briefs, analyst relations and so on.

2. Agree

✦ Work as one team along with your sales group and finalize the accounts that have revenue potential and can be accelerated through the sales funnel stages. Make sure the KRAs of the marketing and sales team align towards the same goals.

✦ Classify your accounts into hot, warm, and cold buckets based on a combination of factors such as engagement, lead scores shared by sales, look-alike companies (companies like existing customers in terms of industry, domain, size, revenue, etc.) and more.

✦ Go back and forth on account-level feedback from the sales team and classify the contacts in each account into the following categories: users, influencers, and decision-makers. Agree upon the right messaging and narrative for each account.

3. Map

✦ Map the pain points identified for each account to your resources and products/solutions. Map the content marketing efforts to different stages of the funnel and build a list of customized content resources/assets addressing those problems.

✦ Estimate the potential revenue for each target account and get an expected total contract value over a specific time period. For example, the potential revenue from an account could be $3 million but across 4 years. Mapping contract value over time periods will help you get a revenue value for the current year.

4. Execute

✦ Execute your account-based marketing (ABM) campaigns — right messaging/story supported by relevant resources and solutions targeted and personalized specifically for each persona within each account.

✦ Run go-to-marketing (GTM) campaigns across identified marketing channels and track the pipeline velocity for the targeted accounts.

✦ Keep pivoting and tweaking your approach until your marketing and sales efforts are completely optimized for revenue.

In the next chapter, we will look at the challenges to overcome in revenue marketing and the phases involved to transition from the traditional marketing approach to revenue marketing.

The purpose of revenue marketing is to build a system that works, and not catering to your preference.

#revenuemarketingbook

8. TRANSITIONING INTO REVENUE MARKETING

....

*Success is the ability to go from failure to failure
without losing your enthusiasm.*

– *Winston Churchill*

As we saw in the previous chapter, you need the core contributors and stakeholders across the company to come together with clearly defined expectations to get your revenue marketing journey up and running.

But as you go further along the journey to make your marketing organization accountable for revenue, you might come across some of these common challenges.

Change Management

Everyone in the C-suite wants to see the proof of marketing making a real impact on revenue. For instance, the CEO wants to know how marketing can contribute to increase the market share, the COO wants to know how marketing can contribute to increase the operational efficiency in marketing and sales, and so on.

So, as marketing is adopting the new norms of increased accountability, one of the biggest challenges you might come across is resistance to change.

© YAAGNESHWARAN GANESH

The resistance isn't just because of the additional accountability, but mainly because the organization cannot afford a dip in profitability or revenue as the metamorphosis happens. The change can be expansive - could range from an org-change of who reports to whom, to the change in KPIs measured for each role, to change in the way collaborations happen and more.

This is a stage where you need to take your customers in confidence and communicate about the change in which you will be engaging with them, and how it will benefit everyone involved. This is important because customers are far more forgiving when you are transparent with them.

This is the stage where you might also go through a lot of changes in your martech stack, change the way you look at data - get rid of a few tools that aren't helping you measure key data points, whereas add some new tools to your stack to make sure you capture the complete customer journey as much as possible so that you are able to measure revenue impact.

It is going to be like colonoscopy — not very pleasant while it happens. But once you go through it — you know you did the right thing.

Change isn't easy, and that is why we suggest involving all your stakeholders to get a collective buy-in.

Driving alignment

Everyone gets what revenue marketing is. Operationalizing it and getting everyone to align is where the challenge lies. Ensuring alignment is an extension to bring all the stakeholders together. Getting marketing and sales to align is an age-old yet one of the biggest challenges of all time.

Marketing and sales need to align and arrive at a common ground as to how they could work together to reach the revenue goals. There cannot be silos anymore.

As a dipstick, ask your marketing team a simple question — what quota does the sales team carry or what revenue numbers were they responsible for?

If you are not seeing a unanimous synchronized response — we have a long way to get marketing and sales alignment.

The alignment is not just about roles and targets - but also about the resources, skills and competencies required to get there. The alignment also isn't just about sales and marketing, but about getting the whole organization — product teams, customer success, customer support, channel partnership teams, and operations, in sync with the revenue goal.

Replacing legacy tools and processes

They say, "if it isn't broken, don't fix it".

But the issue is — you need to know what broken feels like. It cannot be an egoistic approach where you start believing that your approach is the right approach.

As we discussed under change management, you might have to get rid of some old tools, weed out the unused tools and simplify the process, and accelerate prospects through the funnel stages.

The key is to know what to spend your time on.

The list of challenges doesn't end here. But sometimes it's good to cross the bridge when you get there and yet start your journey with some amount of awareness.

That said, to get better at revenue marketing, we need a shift in mindset from the traditional marketing approach.

Transitioning from Traditional Marketing to the Revenue Marketing Approach:

Stage 1

The companies in this stage are not necessarily startups or early stage companies. There are several companies that have been in existence for more than two decades and still cannot map marketing efforts to revenue. Companies in this stage often tend to have marketing teams that act as a service provider to sales teams.

They typically create content or run campaigns in a reactive manner based on the request they get from sales teams. They don't have established processes and tend to have very minimal use of martech. The primary role of marketing teams in this stage of maturity is to create awareness and run ads.

KPIs measured in stage 1: Cost incurred, number of marketing activities.

Stage 2

A significant majority of companies fall in this category. The companies in this stage have a good amount of awareness on who their target audience is, product use-cases for each customer persona and so on.

In fact, there is some level of martech adoption too. For instance, the companies in this category will have invested on a

CRM. But the CRMs are primarily for marketing teams to upload the prospect database and run email campaigns. The key issue in these companies is that the sales teams rarely update the CRMs.

KPIs measured in stage 2: Number of leads delivered to the sales team.

Stage 3

This is the stage where most organizations identify themselves with. The companies in this stage have their marketing plans aligned with business goals but not specific revenue goals. They go beyond marketing qualified leads (MQLs) and know the potential revenue from the pipeline generated. The martech adoption and automation across different stages of the funnel are well in place. But the company hasn't identified the contribution of each marketing channel to the revenue generated.

KPIs measured in stage 3: Cost per lead, potential pipeline generated.

Stage 4

There are very few organizations who are in this stage of revenue marketing maturity. The compensation of marketers in these organizations are tied to revenue goals and is based on performance. The marketing plans in these companies clearly align with specific revenue goals, and precisely know the revenue contribution expected from each marketing channel. These companies typically have great martech adoption across the stages of customer journey and enable sophisticated levels of data collection such as prospect intent and fit data (not just in terms of third-party sources such as social media and press releases, but also direct zero party data[3] collection)

KPIs measured in stage 4: Contribution to revenue, ROI and customer lifetime value.

To sum up, you need to go beyond challenges, start measuring better metrics to deliver predictable revenue. As discussed above, moving away from MQLs is a good place to start and gradually advance to the next stages of revenue marketing maturity.

All that starts when you begin asking the right questions along your journey. In the next chapter, let's look at some of the key questions to ask to ensure you are progressing.

---

3   Zero party data is the information which consumers explicitly share with marketers in exchange for the promise of tailored experiences and offers. For instance - sharing expected purchase cycle information in exchange for access to an ebook.

Marketing tactics without objectives tied to revenue outcome is just like trash talk before getting beaten up.

#revenuemarketingbook

PART III

OPTIMIZING YOUR REVENUE MARKETING JOURNEY

9. KEY QUESTIONS TO ASK AND MEASURE, TO MAKE INCREMENTAL PROGRESS

....

> *Knowledge is having the right answer. Intelligence*
> *is asking the right question*
>
> *- Unknown*

Make sure everything is measurable. Easier said than done, because measuring the outcome of marketing programs isn't always straightforward.

Here are some challenges contributing to measuring outcomes:

Measuring Time Period

Different marketing programs take different time periods to show returns. For instance, a webinar done this month might take a few weeks to deliver results or in some cases it might take a year. So, you need to divide your marketing investment portfolio into what you know can deliver immediately, and some as seeds sown for the near future.

Attribution

Some say it takes 12 touches before a cold lead becomes a prospect, whereas some stats say 6-7 touches. Regardless of what the right number is, we are unable to attribute a dollar value to any specific touches. In fact, the attribution itself is difficult because the customer journey is random. Unless you have a well-connected martech stack, it becomes very difficult to track the customer interaction at each touch point.

Horses for Courses

As marketers, we must target different personas in our target company with different campaigns. There are users, decision makers, and influencers in every organization. If you are into enterprise marketing, then there are even more decision makers and influencers in your target companies. Since different marketing programs impact each individual differently, it becomes even more difficult to measure unless you are collecting zero party data.

On a related note, my good friend and well-known marketer Pravin Shekar talks extensively about 'micro marketing' at marketing conferences and is currently writing a book on the topic. In short, marketing to a small bunch of audience will resonate with you rather than burning cash on a huge audience without any impact.

Here's the link to a video of my conversation with Pravin on how I used micro marketing to promote one of my earlier books 'Is Your Marketing in Sync or Sinking?'

<https://www.linkedin.com/feed/update/urn:li:activity:664852 2869376684032/>

Pravin Shekar • 1st

Outlier Marketer: Unconventional methods to grow your business!

2d • 🌐

#Micromarketing : Listen to Yaagneshwaran Ganesh's approach to book marketing

Key excerpt: "I decided the best way to go about this would be identifying those 10 people who could actually influence your book. And the focus of that was actually to also build relationships with these people. Because if people know you for something, and you can connect with them for that purpose, that is far more fulfilling than trying to connect with so many people and that not resulting in anything." #influence #marketing #linkedin

▷ ◁ 1:13 / 3:41 ◁⑴ [ ]

The crux being – Focus on the people that matter and focus on them alone.

Now, getting back to measuring the results of what your marketing has delivered.

Here are some key questions to ask as you are getting started into revenue marketing. You can divide them into six pillars as shared below:

Strategy – Where you want to be as an organization on the revenue marketing maturity path vs. how ready and aligned is the organization currently, how much of leadership buy-in is achieved, etc.

People – How is your revenue marketing unit structure, do you have all the resources for all the skills you need, have you set up a recruitment program, do you have a program for upskilling and talent management, etc.?

Process – Have you set up a customer acquisition to revenue process? Do you have a process set up for how things flow from marketing campaigns and demand generation to program management and onboarding to converting free customers to paid programs, customer success, etc.?

Technology – Assess your current tech stack and architecture if you have the necessary technology and tools to support the customer journey seamlessly at each stage. If not – have you shortlisted the tools you need? Most importantly check how the technology adoption is across the different teams involved in the customer and revenue creation journey.

Customer – Continuously measure if any part of the customer journey is broken and assess how well the customer data is managed. Are you making sure that all the marketing efforts are on the identified customer persona only, what is the customer engagement rate, what is your NPS score, what is your churn rate, are you able to identify churn signals in advance, etc?

Results or outcomes – Are you able to measure and attribute contributions to revenue at each stage? Are you able to measure improvement in operational efficiency, conversion rate, etc? In short – are you clear on what is working for you and what isn't?

The above questions are indicative questions, which you can tweak according to where you stand in the revenue marketing journey.

You will find the checklist to get your revenue marketing going in the annexure. It is also available in a downloadable format on my website - https://www.yaagneshwaran.com/blog/revenue-marketing-journey/

In the next chapter, let's look at where you can cut costs and probably rethink some of your expenses. Everything in the revenue marketing journey boils down to revenue returns — directly or indirectly.

Asking the right questions is the first step in turning the invisible contributions into the visible attributions.

#revenuemarketingbook

10. CUT OUT MARKETING MONEY WASTERS

Why waste a sentence saying nothing?

– Seth Godin

As we have discussed in the previous chapters, at the heart of revenue marketing is — moving marketing away from being a cost center. Before you get to becoming a revenue center, you need to be a cost-effective center. We saw in the previous chapter that it begins with asking the right questions around what we have and what we need.

In this chapter, we are going to discuss what we do not need and why. In other words, the areas where we can cut our spending, take money away from the marketing line items that don't yield results to the ones that you might want to pour more gasoline on.

© YAAGNESHWARAN GANESH

Getting a budget from the leadership is always a catch 22 situation – we need the budget to deliver the ROI. On an average, and especially during tough times, marketing budgets tend to range from 1-10% of annual revenue.

Therefore, when we get a budget, we need to invest only on aspects critical to driving revenue. We need to distribute the budget between the levers that would augment the existing pipeline and the initiatives that would be critical to the business in the long run.

Always start with a fundamental understanding that it is better to cut the budget than to throw money in the trash.

As we begin to look at areas where we can cut costs, leave out the salaries despite them being the single largest expense. Salaries and headcounts are variables.

Let us look at the other available options.

Martech Stack

While we assess our current tech stack and architecture for what we need, we also need to analyze which tools we can do without. You might still have some legacy tools which aren't relevant to your objectives anymore. Moreover, no marketer wants to log into tens or twenties of tools daily. Also, it wouldn't be far from the truth to say that sometimes people don't even remember all the tools they have subscribed to.

Take CRM as an example. It is not surprising to see some enterprises using different CRMs for different purposes, contributing to inconsistencies in data sanity and visibility. Get rid of the redundant, under-utilized or unnecessary tools that you are paying for. The fundamental step before subscribing to a tool is to think about the potential adoption for it.

Agency Relationships

Whether you should have all marketing capabilities in-house or should you outsource certain aspects of your marketing responsibilities to an agency is a topic that deserves a different discourse altogether which doesn't fit into the scope of this book. But, it's fair to say that you might not find many agencies or partners who will align with the KPIs you might want to measure. For instance, if the agencies you work with want to stick to metrics such as impressions, click-throughs, cost-per-lead (CPL) or even cost-per-acquisition (CPA), and don't want to map them to revenue — you are better off cutting ties with them and identify one that aligns with you.

Secondly, you don't need to partner with too many agencies. It's too easy and tempting to go full throttle when you are funded, but it doesn't make sense to throw money in the trash. For example — we have seen some large enterprises outsourcing corporate marketing designs to 2-3 agencies, whereas the in-house designers are sitting idle. And the worst part is when you have to ask the in-house designers to start the same project from scratch after failed outsourcing.

Booths at Trade Shows

The following statement may come across as bold, but it is worth sharing.

If you are spending on anything more than 10 ft x 20 ft booth, you are probably wasting money. And this goes regardless of how big your brand is.

The fundamental logic is that the purpose of people attending a tradeshow isn't to spend time at a booth. Your booth is incidental. You would be better off spending your resources on identifying who among the prospective attendees are relevant to your product or services.

Your expenses should go into making sure that you fix meetings with your target accounts much in advance to the trade show. And get into the conversion mode. Meaning — the relationship should have been built much in advance to the trade show in-person meet up.

Otherwise, the possibility of conversion from an unplanned meet-up at the booth is miniscule. And it is not worth the $20,000–$40,000 booth cost + flight costs + accommodation cost.

Banner Ads

AdWords, sponsored content, content production and syndication are great. But if you are spending on banner ads, it is better to stop it now. Banner ads are very old school. One look at your analytics for banner ad click-throughs and more importantly its contribution to revenue will tell you that the returns are negligible.

Outreach without Understanding Intent

Here's a 101 of marketing that people often forget: someone who shares his/her email in exchange to get access to your ebook or whitepaper isn't giving you permission to sell your product to them. In fact, they do not necessarily even have a buying intent yet.

And still, how many times do we see marketing teams sharing a bunch of such emails to Sales Development Representatives (SDRs) and the reach out begins. Your SDRs' time is better spent on prospects with buying intent. You need to capture the buying intent of your prospect when you track the customer journey. When you share the contact list with your SDRs, share only the ones that are identified with high buying intent.

Similarly, your AdWords spend should be only on keywords that indicate intent. For example, someone searching for "marketing automation" is very different from someone searching for "marketing automation software". The latter shows interest in tools and not the concept of marketing automation. This might help you increase AdWords conversion by 40%.

The key point is – always map the investments to revenue outcome and not leads. Therefore, it's time you audit your expenses.

Cut what doesn't contribute to revenue.

Pivot to something that does.

If you believe that pouring money onto everything is going to make you a marketing outlier, you probably are an outright liar.

#revenuemaketingbook

11. DITCH THAT MQL

Don't be afraid to give up the good to go for the great

– John D. Rockefeller

How many times have you shared a ton of marketing qualified leads (MQLs) to your sales teams and they didn't give a damn about it?

© YAAGNESHWARAN GANESH

Does it sound like a regular day in your life? Obviously, it's because the priorities of the two teams aren't aligned.

For a salesperson, what matters is the accounts that are likely to convert, the decision makers who are in the buying cycle with a buying intent.

And if you aren't aiding the situation, you won't matter to them. Through the course of this book, we learned that revenue is the binding factor across the company. And MQLs aren't helping the cause.

Here's why:

An MQL comes from the mindset of showcasing a vanity number to prove that your marketing is working. For instance, it could be a huge volume of people who downloaded your ebook or a checklist from your landing page.

Now, these leads aren't people who are necessarily interested in your product. You might have spent a few hundred dollars in running ads leading to the landing page, and you might have generated a few thousand leads.

Makes for a good Cost per click (CPC) story. Makes for a good Cost per acquisition (CPA) story. But it doesn't make the cut to be called a revenue story.

Reason: Intent.

These are the leads who shared their credentials with you but didn't sign up for the product. They were only interested in the getting access to the free ebook.

The short-term strategy of accumulating and delivering contacts to your sales teams, without understanding buyer intent isn't appreciated anymore. And that's because though the volume of leads is high, the connect and closure rates are going to be extremely low.

No salesperson wants to spend time on 2000 leads that translates to 20 demos and then close 1 or 2.

Becoming a revenue marketer, it's your opportunity to earn trust and respect across the organization. If your time matters, the prospects you move to sales teams need to matter as well.

> Contribute to Revenue, Not to a Leaky Bucket.

For all you know – you are better off without Call to Action (CTAs) in your content, than capturing leads that are not sales-ready. Instead, you can build a buyer-centric message, create awareness around the problem you are solving and educate the target market.

Your focus needs to be on making the right target people come to your website or reach out to your sales team with the intent to buy. Your lead volume can be low – that's OK if the percentage of conversion from those accounts are high.

But, why stop using a CTA?

Let me rephrase – Use them sparsely. In a limited fashion.

Use them only where they really matter. Like – on a contact form.

For instance, when you create a quality video content with a couple of customers and discuss how a problem was solved, you are building trust and intent within your prospects.

The last thing you want in such situations is limit the number of people watching it by using a CTA button and gating the video. Marketing is about creating demand which potentially translates into revenue.

> If you have a good product or service – you own the supply.
>
> If you want to own the demand as well – think beyond marketing qualified leads.

Regardless of the scale at which you operate, do not directly pass on the leads to sales teams.

#revenuemarketingbook

12. IT'S NOT A DASH, IT'S A MARATHON

In the long run, you hit only what you aim for

– Henry David Thoreau

The true success of revenue marketing is continuous seamless execution. Revenue marketing isn't just about transitioning from measuring the leads to measuring the pipeline created. It is about committing to consistently contribute to revenue outcomes and staying aligned to the organizational goals.

It's not going to be a quick fix. It requires the entire organization to be ready to play the long-term game.

You can build a great strategy, you can set up a highly sophisticated martech infrastructure, you can have the best people on your team – but, the needle doesn't move unless everyone is aligned and working towards the common revenue goal.

Your path will have hurdles, but it's worth going through the pain.

The Eagle Story:

Eagles live up to 70 years. But to reach this age, the eagle must make a hard decision. In its 40's its long and flexible talons can no longer grab the prey. The long and sharp beak that served the eagle till date becomes bent. Its wings become heavy making it tough to fly.

Now, the eagle must decide. Either to die or to go through a tough process of reformation which lasts for 150 days.

The eagle goes to a mountain top, knocks it beak against the rock and breaks it completely. It battles for survival for several days without food.

Once the fresh new beak grows back, it starts to pluck out its old feathers. Then the new ones grow.

And then in about five months, the eagle is ready to take its famous flight for another 30 years

If you want to win and stay relevant in the long run, you must be ready for the metamorphosis, however painful it is.

Ask the right questions, shed the old process that isn't helping anymore.

Align to the expectations from marketing. Stay agile. Stay positive. Keep delivering

Change is the only constant for marketers. Stick to your goals, not to your comfort zones. Be the revenue marketer!

#revenuemarketingbook

PART IV

BONUS CHAPTER

13. TOP REVENUE MARKETERS AND PODCASTS TO FOLLOW

A leader is one who knows the way,
goes the way, and shows the way.

– John C. Maxwell

There's a good old saying in India that goes – When the student is ready, a teacher appears. It doesn't mean that the teacher magically appears, instead it means when you are on the path you notice opportunities and people to learn from.

Here is a list of 10 top revenue marketers you might want to follow on LinkedIn:

1. Matt Heinz, President at Heinz Marketing Inc,

2. Chris Walker, CEO at Refine Labs

3. Chris Mitchell, Founder & CEO at Intelus

4. Dr. Debbie Qaqish, Principal & Chief Strategy Officer at The Pedowitz Group

5. Jeff Davis, Founder & Principal at JD2 Consulting

6. Steli Efti, CEO at Close.com

7. Max Altschuler, VP of Marketing at Outreach (Founder of Sales Hacker)

8. Aaron Ross, Co-CEO at PredictableRevenue.com

9. Christopher Engman, CRO, Proof Analytics

10. Nichole Marsano, VP of Revenue Marketing at PayScale Inc.

Top 10 no nonsense marketing podcasts to follow:

1. Predictable Revenue Podcast, by Aaron Ross and Collin Stewart
2. The Alignment Podcast, by Jeff Davis
3. The B2B Revenue Executive Experience, by Chad Sanderson
4. B2B Revenue Acceleration, by Operatix
5. Growth Marketing Toolbox Podcast, by Nicholas Scalice
6. Growth Mapping Podcast, by Sujan Patel and Aaron Agius
7. FlipMyFunnel Podcast by Sangram Vajre
8. The ABM Conversations Podcast, by Yaagneshwaran Ganesh and Manish Nepal
9. The Marketing Book Podcast, by Douglas Burdett
10. The Intelligent Marketer, by Chris Nixon and Raviv Turner

LAST WORD

Never a dull moment in marketing!

We all have two options – maintain the status quo and become irrelevant over time, or continuously adapt to the new normal and make an impact.

In the previous two books 'Is Your Marketing in Sync or Sinking?' and 'Syncfluence', Yaag and I have discussed enough regarding the ever-changing dynamic business ecosystem and the need to be in sync with it in terms of marketing execution.

Now, the expectation from the marketing team is higher than ever before. Anyone who doesn't contribute to the organization's revenue directly or indirectly will become irrelevant.

It doesn't matter how many campaigns were run, how many tradeshows and events you hosted or attended, the only qualifying question will be – how much revenue did it contribute to?

Your clients, your CEO, your COO, your CRO, your sales teams are all in sync and ask the same question – how are you contributing to revenue?

That said, change isn't that easy. And, I learned it the hard way.

We spent too much time and money on generating MQLs that didn't translate into revenue. It wasn't much of a problem until a few years ago when my clientele primarily comprised large companies and government organizations. But, as I got into the culture, events and music industry – the budgets and the margin for error became negligible.

I had to change the way I looked at the marketing spend because it all boiled down to ROI. The primary job at hand was to convert the marketing budget into revenue.

It was GAME ON! It was time to execute The GAME Model, which Yaag has crisply described in the book.

We started with two fundamental activities:

1. We went and met our client's top 10 customers and tried to understand the ground reality of why they signed up with our clients.

2. We sat down with the customer support, sales and customer success teams and analyzed all the customer wins as well as customers lost during the current and previous year.

These two exercises helped us to relook and tweak the Ideal Customer Persona (ICP) and, make the marketing message more relevant. Most importantly, the sales cycles were shortened.

Together, we had to make sure our efforts, time and money were specifically channelled to those things that were directly or indirectly helping to increase the revenue and bottom line. To ensure this, we planned team-sessions every 2 weeks.

These meetings gave us a good overview of potential upsell and cross-sell opportunities, their strengths over the competition, potential referral opportunities and so on. But what really helped us to move from a cost center to revenue center was – moving away from calculating product-wise customer acquisition cost (CAC) to calculating channel specific CAC.

This helped everyone to stay in sync and work towards a common goal. Most importantly, the team was able to predict the potential revenue they were going to achieve that year.

But, as discussed in the book, the process to become a revenue marketing team is really that of 'going through the fire.'

If you need to become a butterfly,
you need to quit being a caterpillar.

It is exciting for everyone in the company when you promise revenue and bottom-line growth. They would even cheer you until you ask them to change the way they work. As you go through the process of change, you might encounter a variety of reactions – people who rebel, people who see your idea as 'yet another passing trend', people who find the idea of increased accountability scary as hell, and more.

Soldier, it's time for you to gear up and lead!
As a revenue marketer, the onus is on you
to lead your troops to victory!

Build a solid strategy and roadmap. Get all the key stakeholders across your organization on board. Analyze what's available and what's needed. Get implementing – tread carefully yet with determination.

Measure, tweak, rinse and repeat. Work together as one oiled revenue making machine, and do not not miss out on the soft skills needed in this process.

Set realistic goals. Don't over demand from your team – you don't want your valuable team members to leave. Marshal your troops across the new processes and tweaks made to your martech ecosystem. Drive individual accountability.

Take everyone along. It's a journey where everyone grows together. Reward people who hit the targets and the ones who are really upping their game.

It's time. The question is – are you GAME?

Thank you,

Christian Fictoor

Freelance marketing strategist & Co-founder iGNITE! Music

ACKNOWLEDGEMENTS

I'm indebted to the incredible amount of love, patience and support I've received from a lot of people to make this book a reality.

I sincerely thank all those who believed in me, stood by mc and encouraged me all through my life.

The Revenue Marketing Book is dedicated to all my gurus, marketing thought leaders, martech professionals and more importantly startup founders who are building amazing products for the future marketers.

Thanks to:

Naveen Valsakumar, who initiated me into writing marketing books.

Rajesh Srinivasan, for urging me to write a book on revenue marketing.

Pravin Shekar, the highly respected outlier marketer, speaker and the author of the popular "Devil Does Care" – for his highly specific feedback to enhance this book and taking the time to pen the foreword.

Anuja Surve, my editor and a great friend, for being a linchpin in the making of this book. I cannot thank her enough for her patience and for being the final arbiter in ensuring that the book is simple and real for the readers.

Manish Nepal, the brilliant freelance content marketer and my partner in crime at The ABM Conversations Podcast and #coffeeconversations – for being a great source of strength who keeps pushing me to raise the bar, asks the right questions and challenges me to be better.

Karthik Shankar, the brilliant revenue marketer with a decade long experience across brands like Cognizant and HDFC Bank – for being that friend who pulled no punches, gave me honest and constructive feedback to make this book meaningful. He is someone who genuinely relishes your success and I can't thank him enough for his presence and priceless nuggets of wisdom.

Christian Fictoor, founder of iGNiTE! Music and FPI Consulting, whom I call my cross-cultural brother – for always being my pillar of support and writing the last word for this book.

To all my friends on LinkedIn, who have supported me all through.

Notion Press, for being my extended family and exhibiting great professionalism. Your suggestions have been invaluable.

And the list goes on.

ANNEXURE

Revenue Marketing Checklist		
Pillar	**Action items**	**Status**
Strategy	What stage of revenue marketing maturity are you in?	
	How ready and aligned is the organization currently?	
	Do you have leadership buy-in?	
People	Are your teams aligned and tied to revenue goals?	
	What skillsets are you missing today?	
	Have you set up a recruitment program to recruit the right talent to fill the gaps?	
	Do you have a program for upskilling and talent management?	
Process	Have you set up a customer acquisition to revenue process?	

(Contd.)

Revenue Marketing Checklist		
Pillar	**Action items**	**Status**
	Do you have a process set up for how things flow from marketing campaigns and demand generation to program management and onboarding to converting free customers to paid programs, customer success, etc?	
Technology	Does your tech stack have the necessary tools to support the customer journey seamlessly at each stage?	
	Make a list of tools needed to track parts of the customer journey not captured currently	
	Check the technology adoption across the different teams involved in the customer and revenue creation journey	
	Unsubscribe the legacy tools and the ones that are not in use	
Customer	Measure if any part of the customer journey is broken	
	Assess the data sanctity across the stages of the customer journey and ensure a single source of truth.	

Revenue Marketing Checklist		
Pillar	**Action items**	**Status**
	Ensure that all the marketing efforts are on the identified customer persona only	
	Measure the customer engagement rate, NPS score, customer churn rate	
	Capture product usage to identify churn signals in advance	
Results/ Outcome	Measure and attribute contributions to revenue at each stage	
	Measure improvement in operational efficiency by optimizing your channels	
	Measure revenue generation vs. expense for every channel	

ABOUT THE AUTHOR

Yaagneshwaran Ganesh (popularly known as Yaag) is among the top 100 global martech influencers, a TEDx speaker, a passionate marketer and a startup enthusiast.

Yaag is known for his critically acclaimed books *Is Your Marketing in Sync or Sinking?* and *Syncfluence*.

He comes with 10+ years of experience in B2B marketing for martech organizations and startups. He has helped several startups in Asia and Europe to achieve a market-product fit and scaled them to sustainability. He acts as a sounding board to martech startups by being part of startup ecosystems such as Google for Entrepreneurs' Startup Weekend and plays the role of a Fractional CMO for some of them.

This book is a manifestation of his quest to make marketing more meaningful and accountable to the organization's revenue. It discusses pain points, scenarios and offers a framework to build a predictable and repeatable revenue marketing engine that works.

Connect with Yaag at:

LinkedIn: https://www.linkedin.com/in/yaagneshwarang/

Website: https://www.yaagneshwaran.com/

Made in the USA
Columbia, SC
08 September 2021

45117946R00064